HOLOCAUST BIOGRAPHIES

Hans and Sophie Scholl

German Resisters of the White Rose

Toby Axelrod

THE ROSEN PUBLISHING GROUP, INC.
NEW YORK

Published in 2001 by The Rosen Publishing Group, Inc.
29 East 21st Street, New York, NY 10010

First Edition

Library of Congress Cataloging-in-Publication Data

Axelrod, Toby.
Hans and Sophie Scholl : German resisters of the White Rose / by Toby Axelrod.
    p.   cm.—(Holocaust biographies)
    ISBN 0-8239-3316-4 (lib. bdg.)
    1. Scholl, Hans 1918–1943. 2. Scholl, Sophie, 1921–1943.
3. Anti-Nazi movement. 4. Weisse Rose (Resistance Group).
I. Title. II. Series.
  DD256.3 S3348 2000
  943.086'092'2—dc21
                                00-008780

Contents

Germany

- ✪ Distributed Leaflets
- • International Boundary

0   Miles   100

DENMARK

Baltic Sea

Kiel •

Schleswig-
Holstein

• Rostock

Mecklenburg

• Schwerin

North Sea

• Emden

• Bremerhaven

✪ Hamburg

POLAN

Bremen •

Niedersachsen

NETHERLANDS

• Hanover

Potsdam •

Berlin
•

Brandenburg

Magdeburg
•

Saxony-Anhalt

Nordrhein-Westfalen

Halle •

• Dusseldorf

• Leipzig

Dresden •

Cologne •

Erfurt •

Thuringia

Chemnitz
•

BELGIUM

• Bonn

Hessen

• Suhl

Frankfurt
•

LUX.

• Wiesbaden

Mainz

Rhineland-Pfalz

CZECHOSLOVAKIA

Saarland

Saarbrucken
•

• Nuremberg

✪ Karlsruhe

✪ Stuttgart

Bayern

FRANCE

Baden-Wurttemberg

✪ Munich

✪ Freiburg

AUSTRIA

SWITZERLAND

4

Introduction

In the main building of the Ludwig-Maximilians University in Munich today, students come and go in the hallway, stop to chat and flirt, and rush between classes. With their short haircuts, easygoing gait, their book bags and bicycles, the students today look much like the students of sixty years ago.

But that is only on the surface. Looked at more closely, life in the 1930s and 1940s in Germany—the era of Hitler, Nazism, and World War II—could hardly have been more different from life in Germany today.

Today, Germany is a democracy, with freedom of speech and religion. Back then, Germany was a dictatorship under Adolf Hitler. And, as students knew, anyone who said or did something against Hitler and his regime could pay for that criticism with his or her life.

This is a true story of how several students and their teachers did exactly that. As individuals, they believed that the war started by Hitler was wrong and that the racist dictatorship had to be toppled. Gradually, they came together as a small and secret opposition group. They decided to act in order to realize their goals. Eventually, many of them paid with their lives.

Hans Scholl, Sophie Scholl, and Christoph Probst were members of the White Rose, a student group that opposed Hitler and his regime.

Today, the main square of the university is called Geschwister-Scholl-Platz, named for the brother and sister, Hans and Sophie Scholl, who were among the founders of this group, which was called the White Rose. Every year on February 22, the anniversary of the first executions, a public commemoration is held. There is a small memorial inside the hall where students today gather, and there is also a museum and archive. All over Germany, high schools and streets are named for the courageous participants in the White Rose.

Today, the atmosphere is far different from that which surrounded these activists. Then, the activists tried to keep their thoughts and deeds to themselves, not even telling their parents what they were doing—it was just too dangerous. Then, the state considered them traitors. Today, they are considered heroes. But in fact they were normal people with various motivations for their involvement. One thing they had in common was that they decided to act on their convictions rather than wait out the war.

It is not possible to say that those who were executed were greater heroes than those who served prison terms or were set free. It is not possible to know how those who died would have lived out their years if they had had a chance. But those who died for their acts have become symbolic of the spirit of resistance, which is not overcome by fear.

What can be said with certainty is that, together, these activists tried to awaken their fellow citizens and took great risks in doing so. They felt that they had to do something against a regime that they believed was wrong. Some took foolish chances. They had strengths and weaknesses—some that may have proved fatal. They did not all agree with each other on political points. They were not larger than life. And, as such, they provide touchstones for us all.

A Brief History

Adolf Hitler became chancellor of Germany in 1933, at the age of forty-four. His political

After Hitler became the chancellor of Germany in 1933, he began to change the government from a democracy to a dictatorship.

party, the National Socialists, or Nazis, had won more votes than any other party in the election of November 1932.

At the time, Germany was struggling. It had been defeated in World War I, and many citizens resented the fact that the victorious Allies, including the United States, had forced Germany to pay millions of dollars in reparations to the victors. Many Germans

thought their country had been treated
unfairly. When a worldwide economic
depression left more than 30 percent of the
workforce unemployed, many Germans were
receptive to drastic solutions.

Hitler promised to create jobs and make
Germany strong again. He claimed that
Germans—Aryans, he called them—were
superior to other peoples and were destined to
be a great and powerful nation. He blamed
Germany's problems on a tiny portion of its
population, the Jews. In his memoir, *Mein
Kampf (My Struggle)*, Hitler wrote that the sole
purpose of the state was to guard the purity of
the German race.

Once in power, Hitler began to change
Germany's government. It had been
democratic; now, Hitler gathered all the power
of the government unto himself. He dissolved
the Reichstag (parliament) and, after the
death of the nation's president, the war hero
Paul von Hindenburg, in August 1934, joined
the powers of the office of the president and

the chancellor together. As supreme head of the government, Hitler's title was Führer, or leader. Eventually, he would build up Germany's military forces and use them to achieve his goal of building a

When Hitler came to power, he promised to restore Germany's military and economic strength.

larger Germany, which in his vision included most of eastern Europe.

Hitler paid special attention to indoctrinating German youth. He encouraged teenagers to visit the jail in Landsberg where he had been kept after his arrest in 1923 for trying to overthrow the government and where he had written *Mein Kampf.* Scouting clubs, called the Hitler Youth, made special

Hitler encouraged groups of Hitler Youth to visit his former cell at Landsberg Prison.

pilgrimages to Landsberg for this purpose.

Later, these teens would become soldiers in Hitler's military machine. While uplifting German youth who fit the Aryan stereotype, Hitler enacted laws that curtailed the rights of Jewish citizens. As preparation for more drastic measures to come, he began a program of forcible sterilization of the mentally and physically challenged, claiming that by preventing them from having more children, the Nazis were beginning the work of "purifying" the German people. Eventually, the Nazis even converted hospitals into killing

centers where people who were mentally or
physically imperfect—"life unworthy of life,"
the Nazis called such people—were put to
death. Their reasoning was that these people
merely cost the government money and would
never contribute anything to the state
themselves. To make it sound better, the Nazis
called this practice euthanasia, or mercy killing.

On September 1, 1939, Germany invaded
Poland. It was the first step of a larger military
plan to seize control of much of eastern
Europe in order to establish *Lebensraum*, or
living space, for Germans. Slated for
extermination were those Hitler considered
"inferior": Jews, Slavs, political dissidents
(people opposed to the Nazis, such as
Communists), Gypsies or Roma, people who
were physically disabled or considered
mentally ill, and people who might be gay.

Once the Nazis occupied a country, they
started to round up all these so-called
undesirables. They were then either killed
outright or sent to concentration camps,

In September 1939, German troops invaded Poland, the first step in Hitler's plan to dominate Europe.

where they would serve as slave labor until they were killed. By the end of the war, Germany had occupied most of Europe. Ultimately, lands under Nazi domination included Austria, Belgium, Czechoslovakia, Denmark, part of Finland, France, part of Greece, Luxembourg, the Netherlands, Norway, Poland, Serbia, Belarus, Estonia, Latvia, Lithuania, the Ukraine, the western portion of Russia, Romania, Bulgaria, and Italy. Rumors about the mass murder of Jews spread through Europe. Of some nine million Jews who lived in these areas before the war, some six million were killed by the Nazis in mass executions or in the death camps.

Most Germans did not actively resist the dictatorship under which they lived. The great majority enjoyed the benefits of Hitler's policies. He promised more jobs at a time of great unemployment. He told Germans that they were the best people in the world at a time when they felt humiliated and defeated. He nourished the patriotic and nationalistic feelings of many of his countrymen.

But there were Germans who saw through the Nazi rhetoric of hate. They believed that Hitler was destroying everything good about Germany. They believed it was possible to build a democracy in their country in which people of all ethnic and religious backgrounds could live together.

In the beginning of World War II, the German army was successful, rolling through much of Europe with little real opposition. But gradually,

Germany began to lose major battles, and tens of thousands of young soldiers died. At the terrible Battle of Stalingrad (now called Volgograd) in Russia, which lasted from July 1942 until early February 1943, Germany suffered its first major defeat in the war. An estimated 800,000 men in the German forces lost their lives; the Russians lost 1.1 million men.

At that point, even some Germans who *had* liked Hitler became critical. For those who

Russian troops dealt the German army its first major defeat of World War II at the Battle of Stalingrad.

never liked him, it seemed like the right time
to try to convince others to oppose the regime.

As the war dragged on, consuming lives and
taxing the economy, Hitler and his leadership
became increasingly worried about dissent.
The regime started to crack down harder on
critics. It became more and more dangerous to
express opposition. People who made jokes
about Hitler and were overheard by the wrong
person could end up in jail, or even executed.
Meanwhile, heavy Allied bombing of German
cities had begun early in 1942.

It was in this atmosphere that members of
the White Rose resistance became active.
Starting in the summer of 1942, just before the
Battle of Stalingrad began, they secretly
printed leaflets against Hitler, the government,
and the war. Instead of accepting the rules,
they fought against them. Instead of accepting
Nazi propaganda about the war, they tried to
tell the public that the war would be lost.

Most important, the group wrote in their
leaflets about the atrocities being committed

Early in 1942, Allied
forces began heavily
bombing German cities.

against innocent people in the name of Germany. They took a moral stand against Hitler and upheld the hope that humanity would triumph and lead to a better world. It was a world most of them would not live to see.

The White Rose was not the only resistance group in Germany. But there were many more who did nothing against the Nazi regime. Germans who raised their hands in the Nazi salute by far outnumbered those who raised a fist. Those who struggled did so mostly in vain. Their stories should be seen within the context of their time: at first, general enthusiasm and compliance in the population and later, in the face of atrocities and the flagging war, apathy or paralyzing fear.

Numbers can be elusive and unfeeling. But one can draw some conclusions from them. In 1933, when Adolf Hitler came to power, Germany's population was approximately 50 million. By the end of World War II, some 40,000 Germans had been executed for taking forbidden political or moral stands. The war, which lasted six years, cost the lives of approximately 50 million people, including the millions of civilians who were killed by the Nazis in mass shootings or in concentration camps.

Within Germany, resistance came from many quarters: the political left and right; the labor movement; Christians, Jews, and Quakers; and the military, most notably the final attempt to assassinate Hitler, carried out by Claus Schenk Graf von Stauffenberg on July 20, 1944. In reprisal, more than 4,000 people were executed in the following days, weeks, and months.

In all, more than 5,000 death sentences came from the so-called People's Court, set up in 1934 to counter political resistance. And the special courts condemned thousands more, with no chance for appeal. In addition, hundreds of thousands of Germans spent years locked up as political prisoners. But they ultimately went home.

But of the quarter-million Jews trapped in Germany and Austria after 1941, less than 40,000 returned from the death camps to which they had been deported. Ultimately, resisters must be seen alongside the millions of victims for whom resistance was not even an option.

"The fact that there was any significant opposition is extraordinary," comments Holocaust scholar Jud Newborn, coauthor of *Shattering the German Night*, a book about the White Rose student resistance. "But if more people had been capable of organizing and resisting early on, it's quite likely the regime would never have gone as far as it did. The Nazi government was very attentive to public opinion."

Stars stand out against the blackest night. Such a benign metaphor may seem strange for German resistance against Nazism. But it may be helpful to picture a handful of stars, scattered against a backdrop of profound darkness. Such were the members of the White Rose resistance.

The White Rose

The White Rose was a small group of students and teachers in Munich, the city that was the center of the Nazi movement, who wrote and distributed anti-Nazi leaflets throughout Germany and painted anti-Nazi graffiti on buildings in Munich during 1942 and 1943.

The students wanted to awaken the conscience of Germans about crimes being committed in their name and to encourage resistance to the Nazi regime. They hoped to hasten the end of the war. They knew they could be punished with death for their acts, which would be considered treason. They were bound together by moral conviction and friendship.

One remarkable fact about the White Rose is that it was the first, if not only, resistance group within Germany to explicitly criticize the Nazi government for what it was doing to the Jews. Their recognition of the atrocities being committed shows that many more Germans could have known—and probably did know—

White Rose members Alex Schmorell (far left) and Hans Scholl (third from left) were part of a student medical company that was sent to the Russian front in 1942. Their friend Hubert Furtwaengler is at the far right. Sophie Scholl bid them farewell at the railroad station.

what it meant when their Jewish neighbors were disappearing, but they chose to look away. Later, many Germans said they did not know about what was happening to the Jews. But the members of the White Rose had recognized the truth. For the students of the White Rose, this situation—and the senselessness of World War II—prompted them to begin acts of resistance in the summer of 1942.

The main White Rose founders were Munich medical students Hans Scholl, Christoph Probst, Alexander Schmorell, and Helmut Hartert. They were joined by several others, including Hans's younger sister, Sophie. They were inspired by Munich professor of philosophy and musicology Kurt Huber, who was invited to join in the resistance work in December 1942. The movement eventually made contacts in other cities in Germany.

From spring 1942 until they were caught in February 1943, the members printed six leaflets and distributed them in secret. They were initially called "Leaflets of the White Rose" and later "Leaflets of the Resistance Movement in Germany." They were typed on a typewriter and reprinted by an old-fashioned, hand-operated copy machine. Members mailed them from various cities to various addresses, some of which were randomly selected from a phone book. The sixth leaflet was brought to England by Helmuth von Moltke, and copies were thrown out of British airplanes flying over Germany.

Eventually, the members of the White Rose inner circle were caught, tried, and executed. Several others served jail time. Several of those who were involved with the group are still alive. Among them are Franz Mueller, who lives today in Munich, and Traute LaFrenz-Page, who lives today in South Carolina. Both of them served prison sentences for their anti-Nazi activities. George (Jurgen) Wittenstein, who lives today in California, was not put on trial because his army commander protected him. MarieLuise Jahn, who was sentenced to prison for helping the widow of one of the executed members of the White Rose, also lives in Munich. Her boyfriend of the time, Hans Leipelt, was executed for his involvement in the resistance. Although in this book, we will focus on the brother and sister Hans and Sophie Scholl, each participant in the White Rose was essential, and each showed extraordinary courage.

1. A Youth in Germany

Robert and Magdalene Scholl met during World War I, when he was serving in a military hospital in Ludwigsburg. Magdalene, whose last name was then Mueller, was a nurse in the same hospital. The two fell in love and were soon married.

They started their family in the small town of Ingersheim on Cralsheim, where Robert was the liberal democratic mayor. Inge, the oldest child, was born in 1917. Hans was born in 1918; Elisabeth followed in 1920; Sophie in 1921; and Werner in 1922. Werner would die as a soldier on the Russian front in 1943.

In 1919, the family moved to Forchtenberg, where Robert was also elected mayor. In 1930, after he failed to win re-election, the family moved to Ludwigsburg. Two years later, they moved to Ulm, a city of some 60,000 on the Danube river. There, Robert Scholl started a business as a financial and tax adviser. They lived in a large, rented apartment on Cathedral Square.

Sophie was a good student with special talent in art and music. She loved fairy tales, and the illustrations she made for a friend's copy of *Peter Pan* were published after her

In 1932, Hans and Sophie Scholl moved with their family to the German city of Ulm.

death. Swimming was a favorite childhood pastime, and she later became a fine dancer. She kept a diary and wrote letters and stories. Later, discussing literature with friends was something both she and Hans would enjoy. Friends and family remembered that even as a child, Sophie Scholl was someone who stood up for what she thought was right, even if it meant talking back to an adult.

Shortly after the family moved to Ulm, Germany's postwar experiment with democracy, the Weimar Republic, came to an end. The world economic depression of 1929 had undermined the stability of the government to the extent that by 1932, Adolf Hitler and the Nazis had become the most powerful political entity in Germany.

Hitler came to power in January 1933. He eventually established a dictatorship in which he held all power. Even the lives of children were profoundly affected by the Nazi Party's extremely nationalistic ideals. Like most others their age, the Scholls joined the official Nazi youth organizations—the Hitler Youth and Union of German Girls. Sophie was twelve when she joined; Hans was fifteen. At first, the Scholls were enthusiastic members of the Nazi clubs and became leaders. That would change.

The Hitler Youth and Union of German Girls were designed to train young people to think along Nazi lines—that Germans and their culture were superior. In some ways, they were more like other youth organizations,

The Union of German Girls (Bund Deutches Madchen) was an official Nazi youth organization. Sophie Scholl joined when she was twelve years old.

offering a chance for boys and girls to go camping or hiking. Later, the National Socialist youth groups tried to control other aspects of the lives of their members—what young people wore, their hairstyles, what music they listened to, who they associated with. Members of the Hitler Youth were also instilled with the desire to fight for the honor of Germany.

At first, membership in such groups was voluntary, at least legally speaking. But after March 25, 1939, membership was required by law for all "Aryan" youths. By then most other youth organizations, including one called the German Youth of Nov. 1, 1929, had been outlawed.

Although the German Youth—called d.j.1.11 for short (*Deutsch Jugend* means "German Youth")—professed ideals of nationalism and spiritual and physical development, the group also encouraged members to learn about other cultures through music and literature. The German

Youth, which had branches around the country, was banned in 1933. But its influence was profound, in particular on Hans Scholl.

Robert and Magdalene Scholl opposed the National Socialist youth groups but did not prevent their children from joining. Robert Scholl frequently expressed his own liberal views and hoped his children would learn from discussions with him. He was a pacifist who had refused to carry a gun during World War I. He advised his children not to believe everything they heard, and he frequently argued with Hans, who at first was impressed by Hitler and his ideas of German national and racial superiority.

Franz Mueller was a young school friend of the Scholls' who later became involved with the White Rose. He says that Robert and Magdalene had a critical influence on their children and, ultimately, on the White Rose group. "The Scholl family was very important," Mueller says. "I don't know of another family in the White Rose that had such a decisive impact on their children's political direction."

"The Scholls' spirit was very open," Mueller remembers. As an example, he explains that the Scholls admired work by artists who were condemned by the Nazis. "In Germany," says Mueller, "if you admired such artists you were considered an outsider, even mentally ill. And this was the Scholl family."

They had a wonderful apartment, with seven rooms. The children were on the top floor. They had a wonderful library with some

The Scholls admired the work of artists like Paul Klee, who were denounced as "degenerate" by the Nazis.

books in French. Hans spoke excellent French and when he was a soldier in France he was used as an interpreter.

George Wittenstein has vivid memories of Sophie Scholl, whom he characterizes as being "on one hand very serious and yet very fun-loving. It was more than humor. She enjoyed life to the fullest, and simple nature—a bunch of grass or blossoms on the tree, or flowers in the field—could completely change her."

Sophie Scholl was "not very tall, she was handsome, and she was a free-going and moving person," recalls Mueller, who knew Hans better. For him, too, the memories of the Scholls are vivid: "It is not a long time ago . . . for me it is present," he says. "Hans was a very complicated person, very special, different from other guys. He was very highly educated . . . and he had leadership abilities. But Hans did not tell people what to do. He was not so orthodox, saying, 'You have to do this or that.' He saw different possibilities. On top of everything, Hans had no fear. He had no sense of danger. That was very bad. It sounds terrible, but it is a fact. If you have no fear, you can have a clear vision. But it is dangerous."

In Ulm, Hans belonged to a Hitler Youth group led by a man who had once belonged to more liberal youth organizations. In 1935, this man renounced those liberal values and dissolved the cell he had started in Ulm. But Hans had already been influenced by the character of the Ulm group, which was less authoritarian than other chapters of the Hitler Youth. He and some friends secretly continued some of their former activities, while still being active in the Hitler Youth.

A Turning Point

A turning point for Hans came in 1936, when he took part in a large Nazi Party rally in Nuremberg. He had been selected to carry the Hitler Youth flag of Ulm. Many participants were thrilled by the Nuremberg rally, which had been choreographed by Hitler as a

Hans Scholl became disillusioned with the Nazi movement after attending a Party rally at Nuremberg.

spectacular show and display of oratory, pageantry, and flag waving. He returned home deeply disappointed in the shallowness of the movement, with its constant military drills and lack of real contact between people.

From this time, Hans's commitment turned more decidedly toward the secret group, which—in addition to offering camping and hiking trips for boys—encouraged members to explore other cultures, nature, and literature, including books

that the Nazi minister of propaganda, Josef
Goebbels, had burned as "degenerate" in 1933.

Meanwhile, Sophie was still in the Hitler
group for girls. She enjoyed the camping,
hiking, and bonfires. She found the friendships
more important than the political work. So
when her Jewish friends were not allowed to
join, she did not understand why. She
maintained her friendships with Luise Nathan

Hans Scholl and his friends in the d.j.1.11 were
interested in some books that had been banned and
burned by the Nazis.

and Anneliese Wallersteiner, even though such relationships were now forbidden.

Sophie once wrote in a letter, "In school they told us that a German's attitude to his country is deliberately subjective and partisan. Unless it is deliberately objective, impartial, and evenhanded, I can't accept it."

In March 1937, Hans finished his elementary education. He then had to serve for two years in an army cavalry unit in Bad Cannstatt. But that fall, he was arrested and taken from his barracks to a jail in Stuttgart. It was part of a Nazi government crackdown on the d.j.1.11 organization. The Gestapo, or secret police, arrested young people whom they believed were involved. Four of the five Scholl children were arrested that November and taken to prison in Stuttgart. Sophie was released quickly, but Inge and Werner were kept in jail for a week and interrogated before being released. Hans himself was held in custody for five weeks before his commanding officer managed to have him released.

According to family and friends who remembered those days, the arrests were a turning point for the Scholl siblings in their view toward National Socialism. They now began to see that the Nazi dictatorship was trying to control all aspects of their lives.

In the spring of 1939, Hans began to study medicine at the university in Munich. Like the other medical students, he was a member of the Student Corps. This corps was a part of the army. Its members studied like other students, but during their vacations they had to do military service.

Not all of the young men in the military corps were true believers in Nazism. In fact, Hans made friends with a group of corpsmen who, like himself, were critical of the regime. He began to study religion and philosophy, and his feelings against National Socialism began to harden. He and his companions would discuss literature and art. They found they all respected some of the same ideals: individual freedom and responsibility.

World War II began on September 1, 1939, with the German invasion of Poland. In short order, Great Britain and France then declared war on Germany. The Nazis invaded France the following May and occupied Paris, the French capital, by mid-June of 1940. In June of 1941, Germany attacked the Soviet Union, and the war escalated to another level.

With this new stage, Hitler's plans now entered their most destructive phase. Accompanying the German forces across Poland and into the Soviet Union were special forces known as the *Einsatzgruppen*. Their mission: to find and isolate those despised groups the Nazis had selected, especially Jews, and kill them. Initially, these killings were done at mass shootings, with burials in mass graves.

The Final Solution

In January 1942, Hitler's top officials met at Wannsee, a suburb of Berlin, the German capital. At the Wannsee conference, which lasted

At the Wannsee conference, held in January 1942 in suburban Berlin, the Nazis coordinated the Final Solution, their plan to murder all European Jews.

just eighty-five minutes, the upper echelons of the Nazi Party and government coordinated what was referred to as the *Endlösung der Judenfrage* (the Final Solution of the "Jewish question"). The solution was the elimination—murder—of all Europe's Jews, beginning in Poland and the Soviet Union. With this began the operation of the infamous death camps, most of them on Polish soil, including

Auschwitz, Belzec, Treblinka, Majdanek, and Sobibor, where several million Jews were killed in the gas chambers.

Shortly after the war began, Hans, who was still a member of the Student Corps, was sent to France as a medic. After a few months, he returned to Munich, where he continued his studies as a medical student and continued to develop private contacts with fellow students and sympathetic professors.

Like Hans, Sophie was interested in philosophy and theology. Through her family's liberal contacts, she met artists whose work had been deemed degenerate by the Nazis. Slowly, she began to build her own ideas of resistance to the Nazi dictatorship.

An important friendship that Sophie developed at about this time was with Fritz Hartnagel. Fritz was a German soldier, twenty years old when Sophie, who was then sixteen, met him in 1937. Like Hans, Fritz had been a member of the banned German Youth organization before joining the army. Fritz and

Sophie became close friends, meeting often whenever Fritz came home from military duty. They talked constantly about religion and what was happening in Germany, with Sophie trying to convince him of the rightness of her antiwar and anti-Hitler positions. She argued, for example, that German civilians should not donate warm clothing for the use of the German soldiers fighting on the cold Russian front because this would prolong the war. Later, Fritz, who after the war became a judge in the German city of Stuttgart, remembered how Sophie's persistence slowly convinced him "that her attitude was correct. You can either be for Hitler or against Hitler. If you were against Hitler, you had to see to it that he lost the war." He remembered Sophie as being warm and emotional yet logical and clear-headed.

While the German forces were overrunning and occupying Poland, Sophie graduated from high school. She arranged to become an apprentice kindergarten teacher at the Frobel Seminary in Ulm. She hoped that this would spare her from the obligation to work for the state, as all high school graduates were required to do before going to college.

But after nearly a year of working with the children at the seminary, Sophie learned that she still had to do her service for the state. She spent six months in the labor service at the Krauchenwies labor camp near Sigmaringen, and another six in the war auxiliary service, teaching in a kindergarten in Blumberg.

In March 1942, she was finally able to return to Ulm. Then, on her twenty-first birthday, May 9, 1942, Sophie went to Munich to begin her college studies in biology and philosophy. It would be her last birthday.

2. Important Friendships

Sophie Scholl

Sophie Scholl celebrated her twenty-first birthday with her brother Hans and some of his new friends, fellow medical students Christoph Probst, a married man with two children, Alexander Schmorell, Willi Graf, and George Wittenstein. The men were all about the same age as Hans, in their mid- to late twenties.

During the evening, the group discussed politics. It became clear that all of them opposed Hitler and the Nazi regime. Already angry about the abuses of human rights occurring in their own country, the young men would later witness, during their compulsory military service, even more and greater crimes being committed in the name of Germany. So who were these young men who had the courage to resist the Nazis?

Hans Scholl

Alexander Schmorell had been born in Russia in 1917. His father was of German ancestry and worked as a physician. His mother, who was Russian, died soon after his birth. Alexander was a talented athlete, artist, and musician. After the revolution in Russia in 1917, which resulted in the overthrow of the tsar and the ascension to power of the Bolshevik (Communist) Party, the family moved to Germany.

Even so, the family retained strong cultural ties to Russia. They spoke Russian at home, where the children were looked after by a Russian nurse maid. Alexander chafed at unjust authority and developed a deep hatred for the Nazi regime, which defined the Slavic peoples, including the Russians and Poles, as inferior to the Aryans. In Hitler's grand scheme, the Slavs of eastern Europe were destined to give way to make room for Germany's *Lebensraum*, or living space. The fortunate ones would be enslaved; the rest killed.

Of the members of the White Rose, George Wittenstein remembers Alexander as being "the most complex of all because he was torn between his Russian ancestry and his German ancestry. When they emigrated to Germany they brought along a Russian nanny, so he was really brought up with Russian belief and culture."

Christoph Probst's parents had divorced when he was young, and his father remarried a Jewish woman who was persecuted by the Nazis. His father, who committed suicide in 1936, had been a close friend of several famous artists whose work the Nazis classified as degenerate, including Paul Klee and Emil Nolde. Like Hans Scholl, Christoph had to do military service before entering the university to study medicine. He and Herta Dohrn, whom he married in 1941,

Christoph Probst

had three children together. The last was born just before Christoph's execution for his activities with the White Rose.

Willi Graf came from a devout Catholic family whose religious values led him to an early rejection of National Socialism. Unlike the Scholl children, Willi never joined the Hitler Youth, and he was active in liberal Catholic youth groups instead, such as the

47

Willi Graf

Gray Order, which he joined in 1934. Graf had even been jailed for a short time because of his involvement with the group. Willi served in the military through the summer of 1942.

When these young men met in Munich, they had different feelings about the war. Hans still had feelings of nationalism and felt the desire to help free Germany from the shame it felt after World War I, although he confided to his diary that "Germany has deserved this yoke." Willi, who was shocked by what he saw while serving on the Russian front, was already disillusioned with the Nazi regime.

George Wittenstein says that his own feelings against the regime began to take form as early as June 30, 1934. This is when Hitler had his best friend and rival Ernst Röhm, the leader of the paramilitary organization known as the SA (*Sturmabteilungen,* which literally means "storm troopers") or Brownshirts, killed, along with the rest of the group's leadership. The SA had provided the shock troops of the Nazi movement, providing muscle for the Party and attacking its political enemies. June 30, 1934, the date when Röhm and many of the group's leaders were betrayed by Hitler and arrested or killed, went down in history as the "Night of the Long Knives."

Ernst Röhm, leader of the SA paramilitary group

"Then," Wittenstein says, "one knew what was going on." Even so, it was not easy for people critical of the Nazis to find each other.

It was too dangerous to openly state one's opposition, with the possible penalty of being sentenced to time in a concentration camp.

"You had to keep everything secret," remembers Wittenstein. "You could not even trust your friends. I was in a movie theater once and during a news reel, when Hitler was speaking, someone must have made a remark. He was removed by the Gestapo. When we talked anything about politics at home, we would put a tea cozy over the phone so no one at home would hear. It was a great risk, of course. It would be weeks and months before you knew someone well enough that you could talk to them."

Students who found that they shared similar critical attitudes usually met outside the classroom. The students who formed the White Rose met as members of the student medical corps of the army. George Wittenstein introduced Hans Scholl to Alexander Schmorell and another student, Hubert Furtwaengler. "Almost all of us were medical students," Wittenstein says. He first met Hans through a mutual friend. Scholl, Schmorell, and Wittenstein were all medics in the same company.

In the spring of 1941, Schmorell invited Hans to join in some evenings of literary readings that he had organized with Christoph Probst. At first, there was little or no discussion of politics at these gatherings. Instead, the

Christoph Probst and the other members of the White Rose met as medical students in Munich.

students talked about literature, philosophy, religion, and music, and drank wine together late into the night. Soon they were also getting together to attend concerts and to go hiking and swimming.

Traute LaFrenz-Page, who was Hans's girlfriend in the summer of 1942, remembers about the group that there was "a certain seriousness about all of them. But otherwise they were kind of happy, talking to each other, taking walks. I guess we were not that different from young people today, only our fun was a little different. It was a time without TV, without much emphasis put on outer appearance. Nobody really cared. We read together and that was fun. I am shocked by how much emphasis my fifteen-year-old grandchildren place on appearance. That certainly was not the case then. You made your own music or went to a concert if you had money, or you went walking in the woods or skiing together."

Wittenstein agrees that "the group was very fun-loving. Like most people in certain circumstances, the humor was gallows humor. We had meetings where we discussed our ideas, read our own writings to each other."

The friends held regular evenings in Munich with writers, philosophers, and artists. They discussed their ideas with professors Carl Muth, in whose home Sophie Scholl rented a room, and Theodor Haecker. Over time, discussions about how citizens should act under a dictatorship took place with increasing frequency.

3. A Time to Act

By May 1942, Hans Scholl and Alexander Schmorell had decided that some action had to be taken against the Nazi regime. By this point, the students had heard rumors about mass deportations and shootings. But they probably did not know the full extent of everything that was going on in the lands occupied by Germany—Greater Germany, as the Nazis referred to it.

By then, Jews in occupied territories were being deported in large numbers to the death camps. In Germany itself, more than 300,000 Jews had been forced into emigration. (In 1933, at the start of the Hitler regime, there were approximately 500,000 Jews in Germany. They made up 1 percent of the population.) By the spring of 1942, plans had been made to ship the remaining German Jews to the "east" for "special treatment," which meant extermination.

The war was not going so well for Germany. A year had passed since Germany had attacked the Soviet Union, and the series of stunningly quick victories that the German armed forces had first achieved had come to an end. For most Germans, it was hard to learn the truth about how the war was going because it was

By the spring of 1942, more than 300,000 German Jews had been forced into emigration.

strictly forbidden to listen to foreign radio broadcasts. Within Germany, official broadcasts were completely controlled by the Nazi Ministry of Propaganda. These stations told the people what the government wanted them to hear: that Germany was winning.

Meanwhile, some public dissent had arisen. In August 1941, Clemens Count von Galen, the Catholic bishop of Muenster, delivered a sermon attacking the Nazi euthanasia program, which had begun in 1939. In his sermon, the bishop spoke about what he called each individual's "obligations of conscience," which he said required them to oppose the taking of innocent life, even if such opposition cost them their own life.

"They were the first gassings," Franz Mueller says about the euthanasia program the bishop had condemned. Mueller remembers that in September 1941, he helped a school friend in Ulm, Heinz Brenner, reprint and mail out two or three hundred copies of the sermon to people the young men thought would be sympathetic.

Among the recipients were the Scholls, and Mueller believes Hans was inspired by the leaflet. "At last somebody has had the courage to speak out," Hans is supposed to have said upon reading the sermon.

"It gives you insight," says Mueller, "about what happened with young Germans of fifteen to sixteen years old." He and some other boys met secretly with a Catholic priest in Ulm who "'poisoned' us with good ideas, very cautiously."

According to Mueller, the priest never said "one word against Hitler," but he managed to get the boys to question the Nazi ideals. "For example," Mueller recalls, the priest "said one day in 1941 that one member of our school got a very high medal for courage at the front somewhere. The priest asked, 'Is courage what Aristotle described: living for your killing instincts, joy in fight and killing?' He said, 'You can only be courageous if you fight for a value. And what are the values here?'"

They talked for hours. "We learned to discuss," says Mueller. "And in a dictatorship, discussion is not allowed. It was an enormous training in free thinking and free discussion, and in laughing about the Nazis' ridiculous spectacular public events, with flags and marching and singing. Suddenly we had another view of the Nazis. If you are influenced by such fundamentals, you start thinking on your own, for example, with what the Nazis called the 'Jewish question.'"

The students who formed the White Rose questioned the Nazis' ideals and ridiculed their grand public displays and rallies.

Although the Nazis falsely blamed all of Germany's problems on its Jewish population, Hans and his friends, Mueller says, knew that "all human beings are created by God. That was very clear for us . . . If you have this kind of influence, you get other eyes. You saw things that others didn't see because they didn't want to open their eyes."

Mueller and his friends wanted to do something against the dictatorship, and through their friends, the Scholls, they became involved in the White Rose. They knew it was risky. As Mueller's friend Heinz Brenner explained to him in a letter from the Russian front at the end of 1941: "We have a fifty-fifty chance to survive the Nazis and the war. On the other hand, there is a 50 percent chance we will be killed by being and acting against Hitler. It is no question that our death only makes sense if we are fighting against Hitler and not for him in Russia." Five months later, Mueller, too, was sent to the front. In the meantime, he became involved with the White Rose.

The White Rose

The students formed the White Rose movement in Munich in June of 1942. They decided to express their views in leaflets. The first goal of their campaign was to spread the word that there were Germans who were opposed to Hitler. They knew they could not overthrow the government, and they did not encourage a revolution. But they could spread information and encourage other Germans to question the dictatorship.

"It was not a political organization you could join," says Wittenstein. "It was a group of personal friends with shared interests."

Hans Scholl and Alexander Schmorell prepared the first leaflet. It was distributed on June 6, 1942, under the title "Leaflets of the White Rose." It criticized Germans who passively accepted Hitler's regime and urged them to passively resist the Nazis instead. The leaflet begins:

Nothing is less worthy of a civilized people than to let themselves be governed—without resistance—by an irresponsible and base clique. Is not every honest German today ashamed of his government? And who among us can guess the dimensions of the shame that will engulf us and our children, when the veil falls from our eyes one day and the most gruesome and immeasurable crimes come to light?

—excerpt from the first leaflet

Less than a year later, after he had been arrested and was being interrogated by the Gestapo, Hans said that as a German citizen he felt a duty to act against the government that was committing crimes against people in occupied countries. He wanted to reach the academic community, whom he believed had a greater responsibility to inspire others or challenge them out of their complacency. He believed it was important to shorten the war so Europe could be rebuilt and Germany could become a democracy. He said he had acted as a citizen of the state who was concerned with its fate.

In the first leaflet, Hans wrote, "Few have recognized the threat of ruin, and for those who have, the reward for their heroic warning was death." He could not know that he himself would pay with his life for his warning. The first leaflet, as well as future ones, closed with the words, "We ask you to please make as many copies of this leaflet as possible and pass it on."

The first leaflet was distributed only a few weeks after Sophie began her university studies in Munich. At first, Sophie was not sure who was involved. When she learned the truth, she wanted to help. At first, Hans did not want young women to take part in the risky work. But eventually, Sophie helped prepare and distribute the leaflets. She also managed the group's finances.

"Sophie Scholl, she was the heart—and Hans and Alex were the thinking behind the

White Rose," says Franz Mueller, who became involved in disseminating the leaflets in Ulm, in the summer of 1942, after he had already done some military service in France. "I got the news of the White Rose on the first or second of July," he recalls. He had seen

Sophie Scholl managed the finances of the White Rose.

some of Hans Scholl's writing already, and "thought he must have written the leaflet."

Another copy was sent to the family of the landlord where Traute LaFrenz was living. Like Sophie and Franz, Traute was not sure at first who was responsible. But when she read the various quotes from philosophers contained in the leaflet, she felt sure it must have come from her friends. She told Hermann Vinke that in the second leaflet she saw a "verse from Ecclesiastes that I had once given to Hans. Now I knew. I asked Hans about it. He said it was wrong to ask the author, that the number of immediate coworkers must be kept to a minimum, and that the less I knew the better for me."

Traute ended up helping to distribute the leaflets. Today, she is modest about her contribution. "I gave a talk to a bunch of teenagers the other day and I had to prepare them very much for the fact that I was not all that glorious," she says.

More Leaflets

That summer, before being sent to the Russian front with the Student Corps, the friends prepared three more leaflets bearing the title, "Leaflets of the White Rose." Christoph added to what Hans and Alex had written. It is not clear that Willi was involved until late summer. The leaflets were all mailed between mid-June and mid-July of 1942. By then, about a dozen friends were involved in one way or another.

Now is the time for us to come together
again, to enlighten each other, to keep
our purpose in mind and give ourselves no
rest until the last person is convinced of
the urgency of the struggle against this
system. If this creates a wave of unrest
through the land, if "it is in the air,"
then with a final tremendous effort this
system can be shaken off. An end to the
terror is always better than terror
without an end.

—excerpt from the second leaflet

The leaflets were duplicated on hand-operated mimeograph machines and sent to the addresses of possible sympathizers. The machines, paper, ink, and stamps had to be procured in secrecy. Anyone buying lots of stamps, for example, might be suspected of treason. Alex had bought the typewriter, duplicating machine, stencils, and paper with his allowance money. Architect Manfred Eickemeyer let the students use his studio for the printing.

A few hundred copies of each leaflet were printed at first. More were printed later. Some were mailed to addresses taken from phone books, others to specific individuals at various universities. Recipients also included owners of pubs. Some leaflets were placed in public telephones.

The second leaflet was even more explicit than the first. It referred directly to the murder of "300,000 Jews" and intellectuals in occupied Poland, forcing readers to confront information that the Nazi government would rather they not know.

"Nobody believed what was written about the mass killing," says Mueller. "I think even Jewish people didn't believe it. This was one of the first groups that announced it."

"The government tried to keep this a secret but we knew because a friend of ours had seen it in Russia," says Wittenstein. "He saw shootings and the camps . . . and the chimneys of the crematoria in the concentration camps. He came home on furlough for a couple of weeks and told us. He was shocked."

Before he was sent off to military auxiliary service in Alsace in late July, Mueller and a friend in Ulm helped prepare leaflets for Sophie Scholl to distribute. "There were about 1,000, 1,200, in envelopes. I gave addresses to my friend and he typed it," Mueller says. They worked secretly behind the organ in the Martin Luther Church in Ulm.

The third leaflet called on Germans to commit sabotage against the German war industry. It also proposed an alternative to the Nazi government—a government that would place the protection of the individual and the community above all else. The fourth leaflet, which Hans composed himself, focused on an explanation of the war as an expression of evil.

All the leaflets attacked the Nazi regime and enumerated its crimes, from the mass extermination of Jews and the murder of the Polish nobility and intellectual elite to the dictatorship and the elimination of the personal

Our "state" today is the dictatorship of evil.
"We've known that for a long time," I hear you
object, "and we think it is not necessary for
you to tell us again." But, I ask you, if you
know this, why do you not stir, why do you
tolerate that those in power step by step, in
the open and in hiding, rob your rights from
one domain after another, until one day nothing
—but really nothing—remains except a mechanized
state commanded by criminals and drunks?

　　　We want to try to show you that everyone
is able to do something to help destroy this
system . . . Sabotage in armaments plants and
war industries, sabotage at public gatherings,
rallies, ceremonies, and organizations of the
National Socialist Party . . . Sabotage in all
areas of science and scholarship that advance
the war effort . . . Sabotage in all cultural
institutions that could enhance the "prestige"
of the fascists . . . Sabotage in all writing,
all newspapers that support the "government" and
spread the brown lie. Don't waste a single
penny at public drives (even if they are under
the disguise of charitable organizations). In
reality the proceeds do not help the Red Cross
or the needy. The government does not need the
money . . . its printing presses run without
stop, printing whatever paper money is needed
. . . Don't give to the drives for metal, wool,
and other collections. Try to convince all your
acquaintances of the senselessness of carrying
on this war.

　　　　　　　—excerpt from the third leaflet

freedom of the German people. They contained quotes from great philosophers and writers, including Goethe, Aristotle, and Lao-tzu.

People were afraid to be caught with the leaflets, and many recipients turned them in to the Gestapo, which began to investigate their origin. The secret police were able to tap telephones and censor mail. By late summer, the police were fairly sure that the leaflets were being produced in Munich and were somehow associated with the university.

The police frequently searched luggage on trains, so students transporting the leaflets had to be extremely careful. Often, they would place the suitcase containing leaflets in another car of the train and then sit elsewhere. When the train would arrive at the destination, the students would retrieve the leaflets. Often, the girls took on this work as they believed they were less likely to be searched by the police.

In July, after the first four leaflets were distributed, Hans, Alexander, Hubert Furtwaengler (who knew about the White Rose

In the oppressive Nazi regime of 1942, forced
deportations and police searches of private property
were commonplace. The White Rose leaflets were a rare
public expression of dissent.

but did not participate), George, and Willi were sent to the eastern front, to work as medics. They left Munich on July 23, 1942. They remained there until October. On the evening before their departure for Russia, the friends met to discuss how to continue their activities. They decided to seek new partners for the resistance and had to think about which of their friends could be trusted.

"The experience of Russia was wonderful for us all because Alexander spoke Russian," George Wittenstein recalls. "We made contact with Russian people. Later, Alexander harbored the idea to desert the army and flee to Russia, but there was no way to do it. He was arrested and killed."

During this short tour of duty in the occupied Soviet Union, the young men saw the beauty of the countryside and got to know some Russians. But they also saw abuses being committed by the German military against innocent people. Seeing these things left a deep impression on them and further convinced them that they were right to encourage resistance. Wittenstein characterizes their reaction to what they saw as "shock and horror and rage."

While her brother and his friends were in Russia, Sophie left Munich for the summer break, returning to Ulm. During her two-month vacation, Sophie had to work in an armaments factory in Ulm, where she worked alongside slave laborers from the Soviet Union. All students who were not on the front had to do armaments work. Her younger brother, Werner, was also in Russia at this time.

That summer, Robert Scholl had been arrested for making critical remarks about Hitler. He made the remarks in his own office, and a secretary who overheard him reported him to the Gestapo. In August 1942, he was convicted of "malicious slander of the Führer" and was sentenced to prison for four months. When he was released, he was not permitted to work at his old job.

Neither Hitler nor Goebbels has counted the dead. Every day, thousands die in Russia. It is the harvest time and the reaper cuts the ripe grain with broader strokes. Mourning moved into the cottages of the land, and no one is there who dries the tears of the mother. Hitler gives lies in return to those whose dearest belongings have been stolen and who have been driven into a meaningless death.

    Every word that comes out of Hitler's mouth is a lie. If he says peace he means war, and if he in his outrageous way uses the name of the Almighty, he means the power of evil, the fallen angel, Satan. We have to fight against the evil, where it is at its most powerful, and it is most powerful in the might of Hitler.

    —excerpt from the fourth leaflet

That summer, Sophie was shocked to learn from a friend that for months the SS had been removing mentally disabled children from hospitals and killing them in gas chambers. Sophie returned to Munich in October, at about the same time that her brother and his friends returned from Russia. Now, even more than ever, they were convinced that resistance was essential. They collected money from friends for paper and new equipment. Traute got a new mimeograph machine from her uncle's office equipment store in Vienna, the capital of Austria. Sophie bought stencils and paper in stores around Munich.

That fall, Alex and Hans made contact with Falk Harnack, who was involved in a resistance group that worked within the Nazi government. The White Rose students were eager to make contact with the members of this resistance group, some of whose members were reputedly close to Hitler in Berlin. Reportedly, Harnack informed them there was a plan in the works for an attack on Hitler.

In the meantime, Christoph had been transferred to Innsbruck, Austria, in December 1942 and had less contact with the group. This left Hans and Sophie to make most of the decisions for the group. By then, the siblings were living in adjacent rooms in an apartment on Franz Josef Street, and the other students began to meet there. As always, the conspirators were careful to hide their activities from outsiders, including their families.

"No family knew. Not one," says Franz Mueller. "We had to lie to our parents when they would ask, 'Where are you coming from in the night?' It was always in the back of our minds that they could arrest our families. My father had a heart attack when he heard I was arrested." That arrest took place in February 1943.

"No member of any family knew of what we were doing," agrees Wittenstein, "because we had to protect them. We all were aware that we were risking our necks."

Meanwhile, members of the group distributed leaflets to larger cities in the south of Germany, including Freiburg, Stuttgart, and Karlsruhe. Hans Hirzel took stacks of leaflets to Stuttgart. In November and December, Traute LaFrenz brought copies to her friend, Heinz Kucharski, in Hamburg, who was active with an opposition group there. Later, Kucharski would be sentenced to death for his activities, but he would escape at the last minute.

In January, the five core members of the White Rose—Hans, Sophie, Alex, Christoph, and Willi—decided to talk about their resistance work with their philosophy professor, Kurt Huber. He agreed to help and support them. He wrote the sixth, and last, leaflet himself.

Philosophy professor Kurt Huber joined the White Rose in January 1943.

Huber's resistance to the regime had developed slowly. He chafed at the antireligious position of the Nazis. When he learned about the atrocities being committed during the war, he became vehemently opposed to the regime. He managed to criticize the government during his lectures on philosophy, without actually saying anything concrete against it. Like the students, he was in favor of protecting the rights of individuals—something that the totalitarian system did not do.

New Contacts

By January 1943, the White Rose had expanded its contacts around the country. In February, Hans's new girlfriend, Gisela Schertling, was let in on what the White Rose group was doing.

A friend of Sophie's, Susanne Zeller, later remembered a conversation they had in December 1942. Sophie told her that if she had a gun and saw Hitler on the street, she would kill him. "If men can't manage it, then a woman should," Sophie said. Her friend responded that Hitler would then be replaced by his underlings. Sophie answered, "One's got to do something, or else be guilty."

Early in January 1943, something occurred that helped convince the White Rose activists that there were more supporters out there. On January 13, the Nazi *gauleiter*, or district leader of, Munich, Paul Giesler, made a speech on the 470th anniversary of the university. He told the students in an assembly that women should not be studying. Instead, they should be making babies for Germany. Furthermore, he said he would provide his own adjutants as husbands for those girls who could not attract a man on their own.

When they heard this, several young women were so insulted that they stood up and walked out of the hall. They were arrested. Then the young men in the hall protested. They beat up the Nazi student leader and would not let him go until the women were released. A few days later, Giesler spoke again at the university and apologized. This may have shown the students that their protest had an effect. This anti-Nazi demonstration gave encouragement to the White Rose, but it also prompted the Gestapo to look harder for dissidents. The danger was increasing for members of the resistance.

The last two leaflets of the White Rose were printed in January and February 1943, under the title "Leaflets of the Resistance." These last leaflets were produced in much greater numbers than the first four. Using their new, larger mimeograph machine, working day and night, they printed more than 8,000 copies. Sophie and Traute bought the paper and stamps in different places around Munich to avoid arousing suspicion. The students took stimulants to stay awake. This may have affected their judgment later on, in a tragic way.

The fifth leaflet was a collaborative effort of Hans and Alex. It was brief and offered a plan for Germany's future.

```
A Call to All Germans!

It is mathematically certain that Hitler is
leading the German people into an abyss. Hitler
cannot win the war; he can only prolong it! His
guilt and that of his helpers has overstepped
all bounds. Retribution is slipping closer
and closer!
        . . .Germans! Do you and your children
want to suffer the same fate as the Jews?
Freedom of speech, freedom of religion,
protection of individuals from the arbitrary
will of a violent, criminal state, this will
be the foundation for a new Europe!

        —excerpt from the fifth leaflet
```

The conspirators carried the pamphlets to different places around the country in suitcases and mailed them from different places in order to make it seem like the White Rose movement was bigger than it was. Some leaflets were left in public places at night, while others were placed on parked cars. Later, Sophie's sister, Elisabeth, would recall her saying that "the night is a friend of the free." Franz Mueller, Hans Hirzel, and his sister Suzanne mailed leaflets from Ulm.

A Major Defeat

In early February 1943, the German forces suffered their final defeat in Stalingrad. This was a true turning point in the war.

"After Stalingrad, who could speak of victory, of 'the Führer knows all?'"asks Mueller. "It was so stupid and terrible. After Stalingrad, Germans didn't trust themselves as before. Some doubts were coming up."

The sixth White Rose leaflet, aimed at students, was written by Kurt Huber in response to the German defeat at Stalingrad. Huber urged for resistance to the Nazis and blamed Hitler for the massive death toll.

"There was an absolute conviction that there had to be an end by 1943," says Traute LaFrenz-Page. "Absolutely. If you study the leaflets you can see there was a conviction that there would be an end to this craziness."

The sixth leaflet was written by Kurt Huber in response to the German defeat at Stalingrad. The students made more than 2,000 copies on February 12 and mailed about 1,000 of them on the 15th. The leaflet was aimed at students and

Our people are shocked by the fallen
men of Stalingrad . . . Our leader, we
thank you!

Shaken, our people behold the loss
of the men of Stalingrad. Three hundred
and thirty thousand German men were sent,
senselessly and irresponsibly, to their
death and destruction by the ingenious
strategies of the World War I Private
First Class. Führer, we thank you!

. . . For us, there is only one
slogan: Struggle against the party! Quit
the party organizations that keep us
politically dumb! Quit the lecture halls
of the SS corporals and sergeants and
party grovelers. We want true learning
and real spiritual freedom.

. . . The name of Germany will be
forever shamed, if the German youth do
not finally stand up, take revenge and
repent, smash their tormentors and
create a new spirit for Europe.

Students! The German people are
watching us. They expect us to shake off
the shackles of the National Socialist
terror, just as in 1813 they shook off
the Napoleonic chains, with the power of
the spirit . . . The dead of Stalingrad
are pleading with us.

—excerpt from the sixth leaflet

lambasted Hitler for leading Germany into the tragedy of Stalingrad.

Right after the defeat at Stalingrad—on three days in early February—Hans, Alex, and Willi painted graffiti with tar-based paint on buildings in Munich: slogans such as "Down with Hitler!" "Freedom!" and "Hitler Mass Murderer," along with crossed-out swastikas. Sophie wanted to take part but the men would not let her. They knew that the streets were being patrolled by police. In fact, the newspapers reported that on February 4 the police had carried out a major search throughout Munich for those responsible for the graffiti and leaflets.

On February 5, the public prosecutor for the city of Munich reported to the Supreme Court about "subversive activities in Munich." The report stated that "the perpetrators are unknown. The householders have been ordered to remove the slogans."

The report also noted that, in recent days, approximately 1,300 anti-Nazi leaflets had been found in the streets. Again, the perpetrators were unknown.

"I certainly did not know when they were writing on the walls," says Traute LaFrenz-Page, "and I only later suspected. But my idea to the end was there must be another organization with them. I never knew to the very end that they were the only ones. I don't know if Hans made me believe that, or if I just could not think that four or five people could do all that."

4. Arrest of the White Rose

The Gestapo had already begun an investigation after the first leaflets appeared in the summer of 1942. The investigation became more urgent after the fifth leaflet was mailed on January 28. Figuring that the resistance was using trains to bring the leaflets around the country, the Gestapo started searching trains in several cities in the beginning of February. They put an ad in newspapers in southern Germany, asking people for tips and offering a reward of 1,000 reichsmarks for help in apprehending the members of the resistance.

"They arrested Hans Hirzel first, on the 14th or 15th of February," says Mueller. "He had been denounced by Hitler Youth leaders. During the interrogation by the Gestapo in

Ulm, they asked if he knew Sophie Scholl. When he came out of the Gestapo in Ulm, he saw that no one was following him, and he went to the Scholls. He did not call. He was the first to warn the Scholls. But Inge did not take it so seriously. She thought he was making up stories. He said, 'You have to phone immediately' to tell Hans that the police were on his trail."

Otl Aichler, Inge's boyfriend, called Hans on February 17 and told him he had important

The police offered a reward for information on the resistance. They began arresting White Rose members in February 1943.

86

news. They planned to meet at eleven the following morning. But it would be too late. That morning, Hans and Sophie had carried a suitcase of leaflets to the university. While students were in class, Hans and Sophie placed piles of Huber's final leaflet in the halls. They wanted to finish before the students came out of class, so they ran outside. But when they realized there were still leaflets in the suitcase, they returned to the hall. From an upper balcony, Sophie threw the remaining leaflets out onto the courtyard below. Sophie later told the Gestapo that it was either high spirits or stupidity that made her throw 80 to 100 leaflets from the third floor of the university into the inner courtyard.

They had been observed by university custodian Jakob Schmidt. The university doors were locked and all the students who had picked up leaflets had to turn them over. Hans and Sophie were brought to the office of the president, SS *Obersturmführer* Dr. Walter Wuest, a professor of so-called Aryan language and culture. They were interrogated by Robert Mohr of the Gestapo. Mohr had the police gather all the leaflets. They fit exactly into the empty suitcases that Hans and Sophie were carrying. They were arrested and taken to Gestapo Headquarters at Wittelsbach Palace. Their rooms at Franz Josef Street were searched, and the police found hundreds of unused stamps.

Willi Graf, who had not heard about the arrests, was picked up that day after he returned home from working at the university hospital. Alexander Schmorell was warned by his mother and he stayed with a friend that night who was not part of the White Rose.

When he was arrested, Hans had a hand-written rough draft of a leaflet by Christoph Probst in his pocket. Though Hans tried to destroy it, the police were able to identify Christoph's handwriting through papers they found in Hans's room. Christoph, who was in Innsbruck and unaware of these developments, was arrested the next day. His wife had just given birth to their third child.

The German people are in ferment. Do we
wish to continue to this dilettante? Do we
want to sacrifice the remainder of our
German youth to the base ambitions of a
Party clique? No, never! The day of
reckoning has come, the reckoning of our
German youth with the most abominable
tyranny our people have ever endured. In
the name of the entire German people we
demand of Adolf Hitler's state the return
of personal freedom, the most precious
treasure of the Germans which he cunningly
has cheated us out of.

—excerpt from the sixth leaflet

At Wittelsbach, Hans and Sophie were
interrogated separately for seventeen hours.
They could no longer deny their involvement
after the evidence was found in their
apartment. They each said that only the two of
them were responsible for the White Rose
movement. They were each placed in a cell
with another political prisoner. The
interrogation continued for four days.

The Scholls and Christoph received court-appointed lawyers. The trial was set for the following Monday, February 22. For the trial, the notoriously harsh Nazi judge Roland Freisler, president of the People's Court, came to Munich from Berlin. This was meant to send a message to the public—even though Germany was already being bombed by the Allies, it was still urgent to stifle opposition to the war.

In her cell, Sophie asked her lawyer if her brother would be executed by firing squad, since he had been part of the army and on the front and he deserved that honor. The lawyer did not answer. She then asked if she was to be hanged or beheaded. Again, she received no answer.

Robert and Magdalene Scholl found out from George Wittenstein on Friday the 19th about the arrests. On Monday, the 22nd, they went to Munich to try to get into the trial. The trial, which would last from 9 AM to 1 PM, was like a public event, and tickets had been given only to loyal Party members. Still, the

Notorious Nazi judge Roland Freisler of the People's
Court (seated) presided over the trial of Hans,
Sophie, and Christoph.

Scholls managed to sneak in. Robert Scholl tried to speak for his children during the trial, but then he and Magdalene were thrown out and not permitted to return to the courtroom.

Sophie's words during the trial would later become famous. She told Judge Freisler that what they had done was simply to express "what many people are thinking. They just don't dare say it out loud!" She also told him that "everyone knows" that Germany had already lost the war. "Why are you so cowardly as to not recognize that?"

Hans and Sophie tried to take all the blame so that their friend Christoph could go free. But Freisler interrupted Hans during the trial and told him that if he had nothing to say for himself, then he should remain silent.

All were found guilty of high treason and sentenced to death by guillotine. They were taken from the court to Stadelheim Prison immediately after the verdict was announced. The only one to make a last statement,

Christoph asked to be pardoned because of his three children and ill wife. His plea did not work.

At Stadelheim, the guards allowed Hans and Sophie separately to see their parents. Robert told Hans that he would be famous for what he had done. Hans, who was wearing a prison uniform, asked his parents to say farewell to his friends. He thanked his parents for the years he had had with them and cried when he mentioned the name of one friend. Sophie, who was wearing her own clothes, smiled and accepted some cakes from her mother, saying that she had not had lunch. Her mother said, "I'll never see you come through the door again." Sophie responded that it would only be a few years of life that she would miss. But she was worried about how her mother would take the deaths of two children.

Christoph was not allowed to meet his family. He spoke instead with a priest and was baptized according to Catholic rites. The three condemned friends were allowed to smoke a cigarette together before their execution. Sophie was the first to be executed, followed by Christoph and Hans. As Hans was brought to the guillotine, he cried out, "Freedom will live!" The parents had left and returned to Ulm, hoping to somehow get the sentence commuted. But by 6 pm, their children had already been executed.

Their sister Inge went the next day to the apartment where her sister and brother had lived. She found Sophie's diary, which she took. Excerpts from the diary and Sophie's letters have been published.

The three first martyrs of the White Rose were buried in Perlach Cemetery in south Munich on February 24. After the execution, someone painted graffiti in Munich—"Their spirit lives." Later, the final leaflet was again distributed, this time with an extra line: "Despite everything, their spirit lives on."

Aftermath

At the time of the Scholls' arrests, Franz Mueller was serving on the western front.

Through a friend, he found out about the
executions of Hans, Sophie, and Christoph. He
immediately expected to be arrested, too, and
tried to escape into France. But he was not
successful. On one occasion, when he asked
two French priests to help him, they asked
him, "Why do you want to defect? You have to
fight against the Communists. That is your
duty." The priests seemed to like the fact that
the Nazis were in their country, said Mueller.

The death of the Scholls had a major
impact on Mueller. But "at this time death was
a normal fate. In a few weeks I would be in
Russia . . . The feeling of the nearness of death
was like a narcotic state, a fatalistic state." For
Mueller, death by execution was "a part of
being against Hitler. He brought us to a point
where we could not fulfill our lives, we could
not stay alive."

When Mueller was finally arrested, his
interrogation was simple—fourteen pages of
"no, no, no." The trial itself lasted eleven hours.
"Judge Freisler asked if I survived the trial,

what profession would I choose. I said I wanted to be a Catholic priest. But I really wanted to study medicine. It was a primitive reaction because it meant I was not on his side. He was surprised. He paused and then said, 'Everyone can get into any profession in this state, but not with what you have done.'"

In the weeks following the execution of the Scholls and Christoph, there were a series of arrests. Alex tried to escape to Switzerland but returned because of deep snow. He was betrayed by a former girlfriend while in a shelter during an air raid in Munich. Also arrested were Traute LaFrenz, Eugen Grimminger, Falk Harnack, and several others who had helped the White Rose. They were taken to Wittelsbach Palace.

On April 19, 1943, the same judge, Roland Freisler, tried Professor Huber, Alexander Schmorell, and Willi Graf. Another eleven friends were accused because they allegedly knew about the leaflets. The trial lasted fourteen hours. Huber, Schmorell, and Graf were sentenced to death that day. Ten others were sentenced to jail terms. Eugen Grimminger: ten years. Traute LaFrenz: one year. Harnack was released. George Wittenstein was interrogated by the Gestapo and later brought before a court martial. He was sent to the Italian front, where he was wounded, and returned to Germany at the end of the war.

The families of Schmorell, Huber, and Graf tried but failed to have their sentences commuted. Schmorell and Huber were executed on July 13, 1943. The Gestapo questioned Graf for a few more months and then put him to death on October 12, 1943.

In a third trial, book dealer Josef Sohngen was given a prison term for hiding leaflets in his cellar. Set free were architect Manfred Eickemeyer, accused of letting the group meet in his office; Harald Dohrn, Christoph Probst's father-in-law; and the painter Wilhelm Geyer, who was a friend of the Scholl family in Ulm. In a fourth trial, Willi Bollinger, who had disseminated the fifth leaflet, prepared false papers, and collected weapons, was sentenced to three months in jail.

In a fifth trial, on October 13, 1944, chemistry student Hans Leipelt, his girlfriend MarieLuise Jahn and five other students were tried in Donauwoerth. Leipelt and Jahn had continued to disseminate the sixth leaflet, but they had not had contact with those who were executed. They also had collected money for the widow of Professor Huber, who had no income. Leipelt was given the death sentence and MarieLuise Jahn got a twelve-year sentence. She was freed from prison by American soldiers. Three of the remaining five received prison terms, and two were released.

In the fall of 1943, the Gestapo uncovered student resistance groups in Hamburg. One had used the White Rose leaflets. Seven members of this group died in prison: Frederick Geuflenhainer, Elisabeth Lange, Kurt Ledien, Kathe Leipelt, Reinhold Meyer,

Margarethe Mrosek, and Greta Rothe. Those who did not die of illness and hunger were killed at the end of the war without having been sentenced.

There were more trials in April 1943. In one of them, Heinz Kucharski was sentenced to death. He was saved by a bomb attack that took place as he was being taken to execution.

Meanwhile, leaflets of the White Rose were still spreading throughout Germany and beyond. Copies were seen by Allied soldiers and even in concentration camps. Foreign newspapers applauded the actions of the German students. Did the students think that their goals would be achieved? "It is pretty hard to believe that good will triumph," says Traute LaFrenz-Page today. "But we certainly thought there would be an end to it in some form or other."

How did people respond to the story after the war? Holocaust scholar Jud Newborn calls the case of the White Rose student resistance "a touchstone" for German ambivalence. "Even during the 1960s, while the members were being held forth as shining martyrs, the very same judges who had helped put them under the ax were still serving in the German judicial system," says Newborn, coauthor with Annette Dumbach of *Shattering the German Night: The Story of the White Rose.* "They just retired and got their pensions for the most part."

In 1997, a small White Rose memorial museum and archive was set up at the University of Munich where the friends studied. Books and pamphlets are available from that memorial. The exhibit has been translated into several languages and has traveled to other countries, from the United States to Russia.

What is the meaning of the White Rose to Germans today? "I think most Germans feel this subject [of German resistance] has been ignored by the rest of the world," says historian David Clay Large of Montana State University. Large is author of *Contending*

There is a White Rose memorial museum and archive at the University of Munich.

with Hitler: Varieties of German Resistance in the Third Reich.

"When I hear people say, 'Let's forget it,' I have a horrible view of the mound of spectacles at Auschwitz," said a student from Berlin. "It's something I can't forget. And I try to fight against these kinds of things happening. It's the only way to learn from the past."

Eyewitnesses Franz Mueller, Traute LaFrenz-Page, MarieLuise Jahn, and George Wittenstein are not young anymore, although their memories of their friends remain fresh. They all have shared their recollections with the younger generation, although for Wittenstein "it was not easy. About ten years ago I began to talk about it. It was so painful to think about it."

Timeline

January 1933   Adolf Hitler is appointed
chancellor (prime minister)
of Germany.

March 1933   Hitler assumes dictatorial powers.
First concentration camp opens
at Dachau.

August 1934   Hitler becomes commander in chief
of the German armed forces.

November 1935   The Nuremberg laws are passed.
Jews are stripped of their rights as
German citizens.

July 1937   The Buchenwald concentration
camp opens.

November 1938   During *Kristallnacht*, the "Night of
Broken Glass," government-organized
riots destroy Jewish homes, shops,
and synagogues.

September 1939	German troops invade Poland, beginning World War II.
April 1940	The Auschwitz concentration camp opens.
September 1941	German Jews are ordered to wear yellow stars. Mass deportations to concentration camps begin.
January 1942	The Wannsee conference determines that the Final Solution for the Jewish people is to be mass extermination.
June 1944	Allied forces invade Normandy.
February 1945	Auschwitz is abandoned by the Germans and captured by the Russians.
April 1945	American troops liberate Buchenwald and Dachau. Hitler commits suicide.
May 1945	Germany surrenders.
November 1945	The Nuremberg trials begin.

Glossary

Einsatzgruppen
Special units of the German armed forces charged
with finding and killing Jews and other
undesirable groups in the territories occupied
by the German army.

euthanasia
"Mercy killing." The practice of killing those
individuals who are judged incapable of living
worthwhile lives.

Führer
Literally, the "Leader," the supreme head of the
German government, who held absolute
power. The position held by Adolf Hitler from
1933 to 1945.

Gestapo
The German secret police, charged with locating and
arresting Jews, political dissidents, and other
opponents of the Nazi Party.

Lebensraum

"Living space." The Nazi slogan associated with the belief that the inferior peoples of eastern Europe should be cleared away to make room for German expansion.

National Socialist

The political party of Adolf Hitler, known less formally as the Nazi Party, which advocated the rearmament of Germany after World War I and the racial superiority of the German people.

Reichstag

The German parliament, or legislature, dissolved by Hitler in 1933.

SA (Sturmabteilungen)

Storm Troopers, or SA or Brownshirts. Uniformed thugs under the control of the Nazi Party, used to incite street demonstrations and attack the Party's opponents. Hitler destroyed the SA after taking power.

For Further Reading

Dumback, Annette, and Jud Newborn. *Shattering the German Night: The Story of the White Rose.* Boston: Little, Brown, 1986.

Hanser, Richard. *A Noble Treason: The Revolt of the Munich Students against Hitler.* New York: Putnam, 1979.

Jens, Inge, ed. *At the Heart of the White Rose: Letters and Diaries of Hans and Sophie Scholl.* New York: Harper & Row, 1987.

Keneally, Thomas. *Schindler's List.* New York: Simon & Schuster, 1982.

Leuner, H.D. *When Compassion Was a Crime: Germany's Silent Heroes 1933–1945.* London: Wolf, 1966.

Scholl, Inge. *Six Against Tyranny.* Translated from the German by Cyrus Brooks. London: J. Murray, 1955.

Scholl, Inge. *Students Against Tyranny: The Resistance of the White Rose. Munich, 1942–1943.* Translated from the German by Arthur R. Schultz. Middletown, CT: Wesleyan University Press, 1970.

Scholl, Inge. *The White Rose: Munich 1942–1943.* Middletown, CT: Wesleyan University Press, 1983.

Vinke, Hermann. *The Short Life of Sophie Scholl.* Translated from the German by Hedwig Pachter. New York: Harper & Row, 1984.

Index

Hitler, Adolph, 5, 13, 15, 19, 31, 34,
39, 46, 49, 54
indoctrination of youth by,
11–12
opposition to, 6, 16–19, 20,
42, 44, 50, 57, 59, 60, 72,
74, 77, 81, 83, 95
rise to power, 8–11, 28
Hitler Youth, 11–12, 29–30, 34, 47, 85
Huber, Kurt, 24, 76, 81, 87, 96–97, 98

I
Italy, 14

J
Jahn, MarieLuise, 25, 98, 101
Jews, 10, 12, 13, 15, 20–21, 22, 23,
36–37, 39, 40–41, 46,
54–55, 58–59, 66, 67

K
Kucharski, Heinz, 75, 99

L
LaFrenz-Page, Traute, 25, 52,
63–64, 74, 75, 79, 81, 84,
96, 97, 99, 101
Landsberg Prison, 11–12
Latvia, 14
leaflets, excerpts from, 61, 65, 68,
73, 79, 82, 89
Lebensraum, 13, 46
Leipelt, Hans, 25, 98
Lithuania, 14
Luxembourg, 14

M
Majdanek, 41
Mein Kampf, 10, 11
Mueller, Franz, 25, 31–32, 33–34,
56–59, 63, 66, 67, 75, 80,
85–86, 94–96, 101

N
nationalism, 15, 28, 30, 31, 48
Nazi Ministry of Propaganda, 56
Nazis/Nazism, 5, 9, 12–15, 17,
19–21, 22, 28–29, 32, 34,

37–39, 40–41, 44–45,
46–47, 48–50, 54, 56,
57–59, 66, 67, 74, 76,
77–78, 83, 90, 95
Netherlands, 14
Newborn, Jud, 21, 99–100
"Night of the Long Knives," 49
Norway, 14
Nuremberg rally, 34–35

P
patriotism, 15
People's Court, 20, 90
Poland, 13, 14, 39, 40, 41, 42, 66
Probst, Christoph, 24, 44, 46–47,
51, 64, 74, 76, 88, 90, 92,
93–94, 95, 96, 97

R
Reichstag, 10
Röhm, Ernst, 49
Romania, 14
Russia, 14, 16, 45, 66, 71, 72, 95
Russian front, 26, 42, 48, 59, 64

S
Schertling, Gisela, 77
Schmorell, Alexander, 24, 44,
45–46, 50, 51, 54, 60,
62–63, 64, 65, 69–70, 71,
74, 76, 79, 83, 88, 96–97
Scholl, Elisabeth, 26, 80
Scholl, Hans, 7, 33–34, 41, 44, 48,
57, 59
arrest and trial of (1942),
86–93
arrest of (1937), 37–38
childhood of, 26–29, 31
execution of, 93–94, 95, 96
as member of Hitler Youth,
29, 34–35
as member of the White Rose,
24, 25, 50–52, 54, 60–64,
67, 74, 76, 77, 79, 83, 84
military service of, 37, 38, 41,
47, 69–71
Scholl, Inge, 26, 37, 86, 94

Credits

About the Author

Toby Axelrod was a 1997–98 Fulbright scholar and award-winning journalist for the *New York Jewish Week*. Born in Queens, New York, she studied at Vassar College and the Columbia University Graduate School of Journalism. She is currently writing a book about how young Germans are confronting their own family involvement in Nazi crimes.

Series Design
Cynthia Williamson

Layout
Laura Murawski